BEADLE'S

DIME SERIES.

THE
NEW HOUSE
THAT
JACK BUILT
ATLANTIC OCEAN

THE

NEW HOUSE

THAT

JACK BUILT.

AN ORIGINAL AMERICAN VERSION.

BY L. WHITEHEAD, (SR)

Designs by H. L. Stephens and G. G. White.

NEW YORK:
BEADLE AND COMPANY, PUBLISHERS,
118 WILLIAM STREET.

ALVORD, PRINTER.

TO THOSE,
WHO,
LOVING THEIR BELOVED WELL,
LOVE THEIR
COUNTRY NONE THE LESS,
THIS WEDDING
OF THE OLD AND THE NEW
IS ADDRESSED:

TO THOSE,
WHO,
LOVING THE RIGHT AND TRUE,
HATING WRONG
AND
SCORNING ALL SUBSERVIENCY TO PRIDE,
THIS TRIBUTE
TO
PATRIOTISM AND FREE LABOR
IS DEDICATED.

THIS IS JACK, THE LABORER.

He has worked with his muscles, his brain and his pen,
For ages, to ransom the children of men.
Reformer in politics, morals, and law,
The noblest example the world ever saw.
The true type of progress for each generation,
He works out his problems in every nation.
For every man he does what he can,
And never diverges one jot from his plan;
He lays his foundation in human equality,
And this, he affirms, is the only right polity.
To old Plymouth Rock, with the Pilgrims he came,
And the wilderness echoed the notes of his fame;
And he worked with a will, till the top-stone was laid,
In the Temple of Freedom, the house he had made.

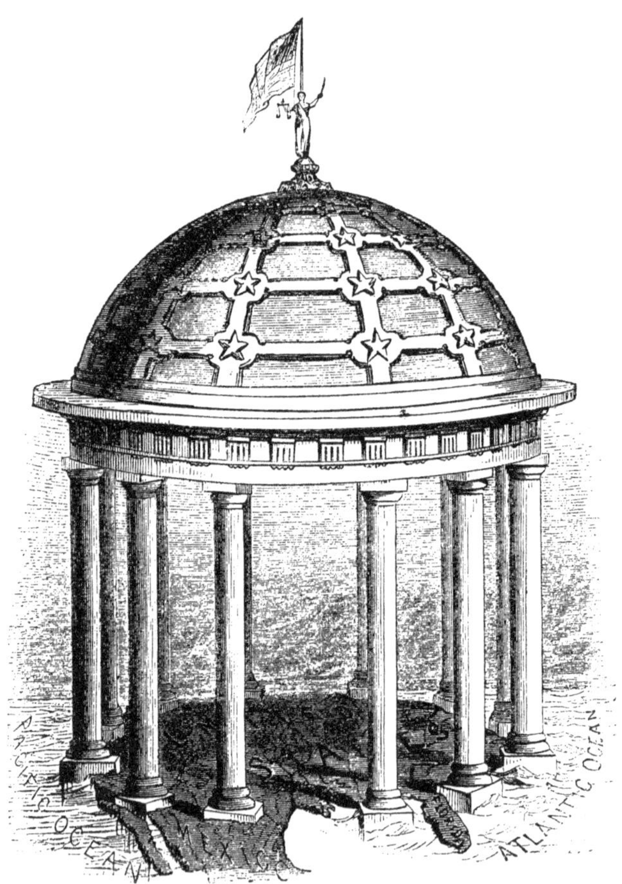

THIS IS THE HOUSE THAT JACK BUILT

A TENEMENT House, on a NATIONAL plan,
So Jack had designed, ere the House he began;
And so deep, and so wide did he lay the foundation,
That it took half the continent for its location.
No matter; the larger the better, thought Jack,
For millions of Freemen will soon find the track
Of Human Redemption out here in the West,
Where, free from oppression, the weary may rest.
So, up went the Pillars, from ocean to ocean,
And, out spread the Roof-Tree midst wildest commotion;
A glorious banner then waved from its dome!
And LIBERTY shouted: "This, *this* is my home!"

THIS IS THE MALT THAT LAY IN THE HOUSE THAT JACK BUILT.

THE freedom of Labor, the freedom of Speech,
Is the gift of the nation, to all and to each;
While, to worship his God, in the way he may choose,
Is secured by law, to both Gentiles and Jews.
A plow-boy may rise to the highest position,
And sanctify effort in every condition.
Truth, virtue, and knowledge, with science and art,
Each ply their vocation, some gift to impart,
That all may contribute, each one in his measure,
A tithe of his wealth to the national treasure.

This is the Rat, that Ate the Malt that Lay in the House that Jack Built.

HE entered the Temple, a thief in disguise,
And he glared on the treasure, with envious eyes;
He flew at Free Labor, with terrible spite,
And thought to destroy its charms with a bite;
With the jaws of Oppression he snapped quick and fast,
And Slavery's poison around him he cast;
Free speech, nor free press, nor a free institution,
Escaped the vile curse of the creature's pollution;
So the Rat he grew fat on the plenty around him,
And thought he had triumphed: the rascal! confound
him!

THIS IS THE CAT, THAT KILLED THE RAT, THAT ATE THE MALT, THAT LAY IN THE HOUSE THAT JACK BUILT.

Some said that it was not a Rat, they were sure,
But an angel of mercy, to comfort God's poor—
Sent hither, by Heaven, to do its decrees,
And serve the exclusives, the great F. F. V.'s;
But the Cat declared plainly, with old-fashioned truth,
That he knew 'twas a rat, by its venomous tooth;
He had seen it in Egypt, in England and France,
Yea, all o'er the world it had led him a dance;
And now, having found him again on his track,
Out! out! went his claws, and up! up! went his back;
His hairs stood like bristles, and he wag'd his huge tail,
As a farmer swings round him his old-fashioned flail;
One bound and one grip, and the Rat was "non est,"
For Tabby too tightly his throttle had pressed!

This is the Dog, that Worried the Cat, that Killed the Rat, that Ate the Malt that Lay in the House that Jack Built.

A QUARRELSOME, snarling, aristocrat cur,
'Way down in the South, you may safely infer,
Disgusted with Tabby, now raised quite a fuss,
And blustered and swore he would kick up a muss;
He foamed at the mouth, and he shouted "Secession!"
Till curdom reëchoed the hateful expression.
At length so excited the whiffet became,
It was thought by his friends that the dog was insane!
But, when he saw pussy his rage knew no limit;
It drove him stark mad in the very same minute;
He vowed with the shackles of Slavery to bind her,
And worried the Cat wheresoe'er he could find her.
Nay, more: in his madness, with fire and with sword,
He swore not to stop till the last drop was poured,
From the cup of his fury, on Temple and Nation
And Moloch rejoiced in the horrid oblation.

THIS IS THE COW WITH THE CRUMPLED HORN, THAT TOSSED THE DOG, THAT WORRIED THE CAT, THAT KILLED THE RAT, THAT ATE THE MALT, THAT LAY IN THE HOUSE THAT JACK BUILT.

Of American breed, and the purest extraction,
She roamed o'er the pasture, and cared not a fraction
What Cow, beside her, cropped the rich, flowery mead,
Or drank of the stream which her thirst had relieved;
'Twas nothing to her how many, beside her,
Partook of the good Heaven had not denied her!
Sheep, Horses and Oxen—nay, even the Ass,
Though Southern, was welcome to crop the sweet grass.
With such a fine temper her coat was like silk,
And she yielded the richest abundance of milk.
Now it happened, one day, that the ill-favored hound
Was worrying pussy, who refuge had found
Near the Cow, who good-naturedly looked up, to view
What was passing—as cows very naturally do—
When she saw at a glance the true state of the case,
And she told the Dog plainly he'd soon end his race
Unless he desisted to torture and plot
The ruin of each beast in the National Lot.
But the Dog was transformed! and a demon was there,
Incarnate and hidden, beneath the whelp's hair;
Divinity issued its fiat of Fate,
And the dog-fiend stood ready to launch forth its hate.
With demoniac rage, and a terrible roar,
That none but a fiend ever uttered before,
He sprung to his work of destruction and death,
Intending to finish it up with a breath!
But the Cow made a bow at the game he was trying,
Put her horns to his ribs, and then—sent him up-flying!

This is the Maiden all Forlorn, that Milked the Cow with the Crumpled Horn, that Tossed the Dog, that Worried the Cat, that Killed the Rat, that Ate the Malt, that Lay in the House that Jack Built.

No marvel that sorrow and sadness oppress her—
That the loss of her loved ones should grieve and distress her;
Or that, like Rachel of old, with her desolate lot,
She refuses all comfort because they are not:
She weeps for the thousands led out to the slaughter,
Whose life-blood hath flowed as a fountain of water.
"What tho' the base cohorts of treason are routed?
"What tho' the false claims of disunion are scouted?
" My brothers, my kinsmen, oh, where have they fled?"
Thus the maiden forlorn vents her grief for the dead.
Lift thy head, thou fair Goddess of Liberty! See!
The Temple is saved by the *blood* of the FREE!
And sanctified over, a thousand times more,
With the blood-sprinkled SEAL on the posts of the door—
A sweet-smelling savor of incense divine,
For the Holy of Holies, the Patriot's shrine.
Now draw the rich nourishment freely, sweet maid!
Immense as the cost is, do not be afraid;
The stream inexhaustible, now, at thy will,
Shall flow like a river, the Temple to fill,
And the world shall acknowledge that FREEMEN can keep,
With dignified firmness, the harvest they reap!

This is the Man, all Tattered and Torn, that Kissed the Maiden all Forlorn, that Milked the Cow with the Crumpled Horn, that Tossed the Dog, that Worried the Cat, that Killed the Rat, that Ate the Malt, that Lay in the House that Jack Built

THE wonder is, not that he's tattered and torn—
That his garments are faded, and ragged, and worn—
That his features are bronzed, and his visage is marred—
That his limbs are all bruised, and his body all scarred;
The wonder is, how, in such terrible strife,
He has struggled so nobly and come out with life.
But the heaven-born instinct that nerved his brave spirit
A Temple to build, for the Free to inherit,
Inspired him with courage, enduring and true,
That Temple to save and its foes to subdue;
And he vowed that his work forever should be
Preserved and respected, blest, happy, and free!
At the cost of much blood, and his doublet and hose,
(For a man is a *man*, in despite of torn clothes,)
Jack has labored, and suffered, by day and by night,
For he knew that his cause was just, holy, and right:
The Goddess of Liberty smiled through her tears,
As her brave-hearted champion so war-worn appears;
And with mingled emotions of sadness and bliss,
She embraced her young Hero, and—gave him a kiss!

THIS IS THE PRIEST, ALL SHAVEN AND SHORN, THAT MARRIED THE MAN ALL TATTERED AND TORN, THAT KISSED THE MAIDEN ALL FORLORN, THAT MILKED THE COW WITH THE CRUMPLED HORN, THAT TOSSED THE DOG, THAT WORRIED THE CAT, THAT KILLED THE RAT, THAT ATE THE MALT, THAT LAY IN THE HOUSE THAT JACK BUILT.

He comes, and his advent betokens the fate
That Despots and Tyrants all trembling await.
He comes! and the clank of the chains as they fall
From the captive, proclaim him the Savior of all!
He comes! and the doors of the prison fly open,
And the bond are set free by the word he hath spoken!
He comes! and before him all darkness and night
Flee away at his presence! for He *is* the Light!
The altar is raised, and the priest is at hand,
All shaven and shorn, at the altar to stand;
And now, through the land, the whole nation rejoices;
As the sound of great waters they lift up their voices!
A marriage! a marriage! a wedding so rare
The world never saw; and such a glorious pair!
No emperor or king—no hero of old,
Though decked in the treasures of purple and gold,
Could compare in his royalty, splendor and pride,
To the patriot WORKINGMAN claiming his bride.
No queen, though her form should be peerless in grace—
Though the smile of a seraph illumined her face—
Could compare with sweet Liberty, matchless, divine,
As she stood in her loveliness there at the shrine;
And angels smiled down from their home in the skies,
And the bowed ones of earth wiped the tears from their eyes,
And the spirits of patriots rejoiced to behold
The dream of their labors so brightly unfold.
A UNION! A UNION! that nothing shall sever!
Free Labor and Liberty wedded forever!

This is the Cock that Crowed in the Morn, to Wake the Priest, all Shaven and Shorn, that Married the Man all Tattered and Torn, that Kissed the Maiden all Forlorn, that Milked the Cow with the Crumpled Horn, that Tossed the Dog, that Worried the Cat, that Killed the Rat, that Ate the Malt, that Lay in the House that Jack Built.

THE priest at his labors, by word and by deed,
In active benevolence none could exceed;
In season and out, at all times of the year,
If his presence was needed he'd surely be there.
He would weep with the mourner, rejoice with the gay,
And help, with a blessing, the poor on their way.
Untiring, incessant, he grudged every minute
That kept him from work—for his heart, it was in it!

The lark was too late with its carol so sweet,
As it soared in the morning the sunshine to greet;
The priest could not slumber so long on his bed,
For he knew that his Master had not, for his head,
A pillow to rest on; and *he* would not dare
To refuse, in degree, his privations to share.

But listen! The cock, with a shrill chanticleer,
Proclaims, by his voice, that the dawning is near.
Awake, Priest, awake! To thy labors once more!
Away to the Temple, God's grace to implore
On the day—on the nuptials—and on this great nation,
Thus gathered to witness the New Life's celebration!

The shouts of the multitude sound through the air;
The bells peal their echo to hearts far and near;
Haste, haste to the altar—thy vesture gird on!
A nation of freemen to-day are new-born,
And the clarion of fame sends the tidings afar,
That the Right with the Might are triumphant:
HURRAH!

www.ingramcontent.com/pod-product-compliance
Lightning Source LLC
LaVergne TN
LVHW011142110826
845150LV00008B/2463
9781418192990